Food Safety

Fitness
Food & Nutrition
Food Safety
Health & Hygiene
Healthy Diet
Malnutrition

Food Safety

MASON CREST
PHILADELPHIA
MIAMI

Mason Crest
450 Parkway Drive, Suite D
Broomall, Pennsylvania 19008
(866) MCP-BOOK (toll-free)
www.masoncrest.com

First printing
9 8 7 6 5 4 3 2 1

ISBN (series) 978-1-4222-4217-9
ISBN (hardback) 978-1-4222-4220-9
ISBN (ebook) 978-1-4222-7591-7

Cataloging-in-Publication Data on file with the Library of Congress

Developed and Produced by National Highlights, Inc.
Interior and Cover Design: Jana Rade
Copy Editor: Adirondack Editing
Production: Michelle Luke

QR CODES AND LINKS TO THIRD-PARTY CONTENT

You may gain access to certain third-party content ("Third-Party Sites") by scanning and using the QR Codes that appear in this publication (the "QR Codes"). We do not operate or control in any respect any information, products, or services on such Third-Party Sites linked to by us via the QR Codes included in this publication, and we assume no responsibility for any materials you may access using the QR Codes. Your use of the QR Codes may be subject to terms, limitations, or restrictions set forth in the applicable terms of use or otherwise established by the owners of the Third-Party Sites. Our linking to such Third-Party Sites via the QR Codes does not imply an endorsement or sponsorship of such Third-Party Sites or the information, products, or services offered on or through the Third-Party Sites, nor does it imply an endorsement or sponsorship of this publication by the owners of such Third-Party Sites.

CONTENTS

KEY ICONS TO LOOK FOR

WORDS TO UNDERSTAND: These words with their easy-to-understand definitions will increase the reader's understanding of the text while building vocabulary skills.

SIDEBARS: This boxed material within the main text allows readers to build knowledge, gain insights, explore possibilities, and broaden their perspectives by weaving together additional information to provide realistic and holistic perspectives.

EDUCATIONAL VIDEOS: Readers can view videos by scanning our QR codes, providing them with additional educational content to supplement the text. Examples include news coverage, moments in history, speeches, iconic sports moments, and much more!

TEXT-DEPENDENT QUESTIONS: These questions send the reader back to the text for more careful attention to the evidence presented there.

RESEARCH PROJECTS: Readers are pointed toward areas of further inquiry connected to each chapter. Suggestions are provided for projects that encourage deeper research and analysis.

SERIES GLOSSARY OF KEY TERMS: This back-of-the-book glossary contains terminology used throughout this series. Words found here increase the reader's ability to read and comprehend higher-level books and articles in this field.

WHAT IS FOOD SAFETY?

The term food safety describes processes for handling food to keep it safe and healthy for consumption. Food safety must be considered from the very first moments when food is grown to when it is shipped and sold, through preparation and storage. Food safety is very important in all these stages.

 WORDS TO UNDERSTAND

HAZARD: a form of danger

HYGIENIC: sanitary; germ-free

INDIFFERENT: a feeling of no interest or concern about something

PERISHABLE: something that can spoil easily

SANITARY: germ-free

A basic introduction to food safety.

The changing lifestyle of people has given rise to many unhealthy food habits, which lead to many health-related problems. The safety of food is also being ignored due to a fast-paced lifestyle. People are increasingly choosing taste over nutrition. They have less time to spend cooking, choosing instead to eat from the most easily available sources. Thus, food safety faces new challenges in the present times.

WHY IS FOOD SAFETY IMPORTANT?

Foods contain nutrients we need to survive, but they also contain bacteria that can make us sick if we aren't careful. Consumption of spoiled food can lead to many diseases. Consequently, there are many legal obligations, as well as pressure from the industry for keeping food hygienic if it is to be sold to the public.

Further, spoilage of food is one of the chief reasons behind unavailability of food. Hence, the safety of food is extremely important. If food is not protected properly, it may lead to the wasting of the entire effort that went into its production.

KNOWLEDGE OF FOOD SAFETY

Food is a **perishable** product, and it can be spoiled easily if it is not stored safely. This care is important at every step that leads food to final consumption. However, many people around the world are unaware of the basic measures that need to be practiced to keep food healthy. These measures should be followed even if we are only at the consumption stage. These measures include the following: washing hands before eating, checking the expiration date of food items before purchasing, and proper storage of food.

ATTITUDE TOWARD FOOD SAFETY

Some people assume that protecting food from **hazards** is not their responsibility. This attitude can result from a lack of education or knowledge, or simply an assumption that the required measures must have been taken by someone else. The age of the person also plays an important role, as younger people are generally more **indifferent**.

IS FAST FOOD SAFE FOOD?

Fast foods tend to be high in sugar, fat, and salt—in other words, most are not known to be healthy. What fast food does have on its side is that it's usually cheap. But that in itself can cause food-safety issues: the staff serving fast food is generally low-paid, to keep prices low. This cheap labor is not always well trained in food safety measures. Further, ingredients of poor quality may be used in preparing fast foods. This may add to food safety concerns and even cause illnesses due to the consumption of unsafe food.

USE OF PACKAGED FOOD

The increasing use of "ready-to-eat" packaged food has also raised several health concerns. Many of these food items are not as healthy as freshly cooked food items. The possibility of food contamination during preparation, packing, storing, and transporting contributes to this health difference.

HANDLING FOOD IN BULK

Nowadays, we use food items that are available in stores in huge quantities. It is not easy to handle food in bulk, as there could be problems in maintaining the food's hygiene. The vehicles used to transport food also carry other products, and the cleanliness of these vehicles may not be sufficient. The food may be packed using good methods, but the places where they are stored might have unhygienic conditions. Most of these problems are difficult for consumers to control.

COOKING IN MICROWAVES

Many of us just can't do without microwave ovens. They reduce the burden of cooking and are very helpful when it comes to using packaged and frozen food. However, they can have some harmful effects on our food. The process of heat generation in microwaves can spoil the nutritional value of some food items. Also, microwaves don't always heat food items evenly, with the result that not all the bacteria contained in the food is killed during heating.

INCREASING USE OF CHEMICALS

Chemicals are also used in many types of food products. Some food items that used to be prepared naturally are now being prepared using chemicals. This is done either for profit or for meeting food requirements. The safety of food is threatened due to the presence of these chemicals. However, the chemicals used for preserving food items are generally not considered to be harmful.

DID YOU KNOW?

- Fruits and vegetables should be washed carefully before they are eaten.

- Overreliance on fast food is a significant cause of obesity in America.

- Cooking food can kill its bacteria.

FOOD QUALITY

Food quality includes the appearance of food, as well as its texture, flavor, grade standards, and certain internal factors. Food of low or poor quality is not considered good for human consumption. For commercial use of food, its quality must be maintained up to a desired standard. These standards are set by regulatory authorities for the safety of consumers.

 WORDS TO UNDERSTAND

ADULTERATED: weakened or lessened in purity by the addition of a foreign or inferior substance

COMMERCIAL: suitable, adequate, or prepared for commerce

CONTAMINATION: spoilage of a food item to the point where it becomes unfit for eating

GUIDELINES: a given set of rules to be followed

FACTORS TO DETERMINE FOOD QUALITY

The quality of food can be checked by various internal and external factors. The internal factors include the effect of biological or chemical factors on food, which can damage the food quality. The external factors include characteristics of food like its color, appearance, smell, shape, and size. Any change in the food from its regular form may indicate damage.

IMPORTANCE OF FOOD QUALITY

Food quality is important because our physical and mental health depend in part on the quality of our food. Food-quality management has become a major concern of health organizations across the world. In addition to safety, the attributes of food quality also include its nutritional value and functional properties. Good-quality food should be safe from contamination or any other substance that can make it hazardous to the health of consumers.

ADULTERATED FOOD

Food that has become unsafe for consumption is called adulterated food. This adulteration can be a result of several intentional or unintentional reasons. In some cases, the food is considered unsafe for consumption if it contains any harmful substance. These substances can include pesticides, illegal additives, and others. Some food items are considered damaged if their quality doesn't meet the required guidelines.

PROCESS OF FOOD SPOILAGE

The spoilage of food can be caused at any stage of its production, such as preparation, preservation, storage, or even consumption. If the food becomes adulterated or contaminated for any reason, it should not be consumed. However, most causes of food spoilage are controllable if the right measures are taken at the right stage. This damage is usually caused by neglect in handling.

CAUSES OF FOOD SPOILAGE

There are three main reasons food can get spoiled: biological hazards, chemical hazards, and physical hazards. These hazards can render food unsafe or affect its quality, thereby making it unfit for consumption. Some of the reasons behind food spoilage are visible, like bad containers for storage, or poor transportation. However, some of these reasons are not visible, such as microorganisms, or chemical reactions.

DID YOU KNOW?

- Ready-to-cook food may not be completely free of bacteria since it is not always cooked at temperatures high enough or long enough to kill the bacteria.

- Food cooked in damaged aluminum pans can be harmful to the health of consumers.

BIOLOGICAL HAZARDS

One of the primary causes of food spoilage is biological hazards. Biological hazards are caused by living organisms, such as bacteria, viruses, and *parasites*, which develop in food products and spoil the food. These hazards create problems mostly for human beings. *Toxins* created by harmful organisms are the main cause of food adulteration.

 WORDS TO UNDERSTAND

PARASITES: organisms that depend on other organisms for their nutrients

PRESERVATIVE: a substance added to a product to protect it from spoilage

TOXINS: poisons

BACTERIA

The first biological hazard to food safety is bacteria. Many species of bacteria can develop in food items. These bacteria spoil the food by releasing poisonous toxins into it. Food poisoning is mainly caused by the bacterium named *Salmonella*. *Staphylococcus aureus, Listeria monocytogenes,* and *Vibrio parahaemolyticus* are all examples of food-spoiling bacteria.

VIRUSES

The second biological hazard that disturbs food safety is viruses. Viruses can lead to many forms of infections in the human body. Some diseases caused by viruses can be extremely dangerous. The most common viruses are hepatitis A rotavirus, norovirus, and Norwalk virus. Viral infections are a common cause of illness in people.

PARASITES

Parasites pose another biological hazard to food and are also responsible for several diseases. They are easily found in adulterated food, as they grow in unhygienic conditions. In earlier times,

PREVENTION OF BIOLOGICAL HAZARDS

Biological hazards can be reduced with proper prevention. Storing food at low temperature in the refrigerator can increase its life. Keep your refrigerator clean and uncluttered. Cooking, dehydration, and proper packing of food, proper hygiene, and adding preservatives all help in protecting food from biological hazards. There are also many food processing methods for protecting food from the damage caused by these factors.

they were believed to affect food in places with poor hygiene. But, due to the transport of food from one place to another, parasites can end up in places with good hygiene also. Some examples are *Anisakis*, *Entamoeba*, and *Toxoplasma gondii*.

SOURCES OF BIOLOGICAL HAZARDS

Harmful organisms can be transferred to our food from various sources. Water and soil that are affected by harmful manure may harm food items by inviting biological hazards. Food can also become unsafe for consumption if it comes into contact with unhygienic conditions. Contact with infected human beings or animals can also cause this hazard.

FACTORS ENCOURAGING BIOLOGICAL HAZARDS

There are some factors that increase the growth of food-damaging organisms. Temperature is one of the main factors affecting this growth. These organisms grow more in high temperature. High water content in a food item also increases bacterial growth. The acid level of food items also determines the growth of these organisms.

DID YOU KNOW?

- Freezing food only stops the growth of bacteria, it doesn't kill them.

- Use of wooden chopping boards may increase bacterial growth because wood is porous and can thus absorb the most harmful bacteria during preparation for cooking.

CHEMICAL HAZARDS

The use of chemicals is very common in today's world. They are greatly used in food and agriculture industries. If toxic substances are present in large quantities in a food item, it becomes poisonous. Some of these chemicals may be made by industry and some are natural as they grow in poor surroundings. Due to the excessive use of chemicals in food items, they have become a part of our daily food consumption.

WORDS TO UNDERSTAND

GENES: units of heredity

METABOLISM: chemical processes in the body that maintain life

PROHIBITED: banned

TYPES OF CHEMICAL HAZARDS

Chemical hazards are basically grouped into two forms: **prohibited** hazardous chemicals and unavoidable hazardous chemicals. Prohibited chemicals are not allowed to be used in any food item due to their highly toxic nature. Unavoidable chemicals are those that cannot be avoided in food items. However, the amount in which they are to be used is controlled by regulatory agencies. The guidelines for usage of these chemicals should be mentioned on their packing material.

SOURCES OF CHEMICAL HAZARDS

Chemical hazards can come from direct, indirect, natural, and artificial sources. The main sources of chemicals in food items are food additives, chemicals used in preserving and processing food, environmental pollutants, naturally produced toxins, and pesticides.

EFFECTS OF CHEMICAL HAZARDS

Chemical hazards can have extremely harmful effects on human beings. Their presence in food can lead to several diseases. Some chemicals can have fatal effects on human beings. Chemicals can have bad health effects on animals as well. However, their effect on human beings is far more severe than on animals. Chemicals can lead to cancers, disturb the body's **metabolism**, affect growth and development, damage **genes**, and more.

CONTROLLING CHEMICAL HAZARDS AT THE PERSONAL LEVEL

Some chemical hazards can be controlled by individuals. The basic ways of protecting oneself from these hazards are keeping surroundings clean and keeping oneself informed about preventive measures. We should be very careful while purchasing, cooking, eating, and storing food.

An introduction to toxic chemicals that can get into your food.

CONTROLLING CHEMICAL HAZARDS IN MANUFACTURING

Chemical hazards are mostly spread at the manufacturing level. It makes controlling these hazards extremely important at this stage. The chemicals used in food items should be reduced to the lowest possible level to reduce their harmful effects. Food items should also be checked and packed properly before offering them to the public for consumption.

DID YOU KNOW?

- Detergents used in cleaning the food manufacturing area can cause chemical hazards.

- Chemicals should not be used near open food containers.

PHYSICAL HAZARDS

The foreign bodies or items that are present in food are called physical hazards. These unwanted items often get into food accidentally*, but they can be extremely harmful. They can either be present in food items naturally or dropped into them by mistake. Items like fish bones are physical hazards that are present naturally in food. However, materials like glass, plastic, metals, and hair are physical hazards that can be introduced accidentally.*

 WORDS TO UNDERSTAND

ACCIDENTALLY: without any planning

METAL DETECTOR: device that gives a signal when it is close to metal

X-RAY: machines that use radiation to penetrate objects and create photographic images of what's inside

CLASSIFICATION OF PHYSICAL HAZARDS

Physical hazards can be classified into three categories: low risk, medium risk, and high risk. This classification is based on the level of damage these hazard sources may cause to their victim. The objects that cause very little harm to humans are included in the low-risk category. The items that may cause moderate level of harm to people are included in the medium-risk category. However, items that are considered deadly are included in the high-risk category.

DETECTION OF PHYSICAL HAZARDS

Physical hazards usually don't have much effect on the appearance, taste, or smell of food items. This makes their detection a little difficult. However, there are many methods of checking for the presence of foreign substances in food. Methods are used according to the nature of the hazards. Metal detectors and magnets can be used to detect metals. X-ray machines can be used to search for plastics, metals, stones, bones, nails, and so on.

SOURCES OF PHYSICAL HAZARDS

Unwanted physical hazards can come into contact with our food at any stage of the food supply chain. Most physical hazards enter our food during the manufacturing and processing stage. Metals can enter food items from broken utensils or materials like staples, blades, or needles. Plastic can come from the gloves of manufacturing staff, tools, or other equipment.

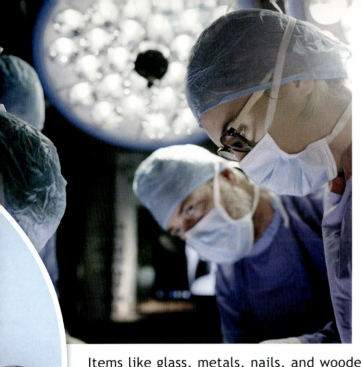

EFFECTS OF PHYSICAL HAZARDS

The effect of physical hazards is based on the level of their risk classification. Biological and chemical hazards are responsible for diseases and infections. However, physical hazards can be the cause of severe injuries caused to human bodies.

Items like glass, metals, nails, and wooden items can cause damage to the gums, intestines, stomach, and other parts of the body. They can lead to cuts in the mouth and throat.

PREVENTING PHYSICAL HAZARDS

Physical hazards can be controlled easily with proper attention. There are many ways of controlling these hazards. These include proper maintenance of tools and utensils, proper checking of material, training employees on checking and handling food items, and others. The machines used for detecting physical hazards should also be used to reduce the harmful effects of these hazards.

DID YOU KNOW?

- Food should only be purchased from approved places.

- In 2008, a man in New York City brought a lawsuit against the Subway sandwich chain after he found a knife baked into his meal. The suit was eventually settled for $20,000 USD.

FOOD REGULATION

Most governments take measures to protect and preserve food. One of the most important measures is the passing of food safety acts. Since food laws are regulated by the government, they are strictly followed. Many countries and even states have developed different food safety acts. Some examples of these acts from different countries include the Food Safety Act, the Food Standards Act, and the Food Safety Modernization Act.

WORDS TO UNDERSTAND

IMPORTED: describes goods that are brought in from other countries to be sold

REGULATED: describes something that is supervised

THE FOOD SAFETY ACT (1990)

This act was passed in 1990 by the government of the United Kingdom. The instructions in this act are to be followed by all food manufacturing companies. They are important for the companies dealing with the supply of food in any manner. The main purpose of this act is to properly manage the food items meant for human use. According to this act, the substances, their nature, and the quality of food items should be properly labeled.

THE FOOD SAFETY MODERNIZATION ACT (2011)

This act was passed in 2011 in the United States. This act gave many additional powers to the Food and Drug Administration (FDA), helping this agency to function more efficiently and pursue its goal of improved food safety in the United States. This act empowers the FDA to make strong rules to govern farmers, manufacturers, and so on. It also helps in maintaining the quality of food items imported from other countries.

THE FOOD STANDARDS ACT (1999)

This act was introduced in the UK's House of Commons in 1999 to create the Food Standards Agency. It also aimed at improving the health condition of people by controlling many foodborne diseases, and helped in protecting the interest of consumers at all stages of the food supply chain.

FOOD SAFETY AND STANDARDS ACT (2006)

The Indian government passed the Food Safety and Standards Act in 2006. This act deals with the safety of food products at all stages. It also issues guidelines to maintain the quality of food in India. The achievement of the best possible public health is also an important concern of this act. This act has been very helpful in dealing with food problems and some health-related issues in India.

CHALLENGES FACING FOOD LEGISLATION

Food acts are passed to help citizens. However, not everyone welcomes them in a positive way. Businesses sometimes don't like them because increased focus on safety can add to production costs, which hurts their bottom line. Others believe them to be tools of the government and rich manufacturers designed to fool people. Some opposition is usually expected since people are generally resistant to change. Unavailability of proper data is another difficulty faced by lawmakers while framing food acts.

DID YOU KNOW?

- The food safety acts make selling of unsafe food illegal.

- Around 80 million Americans are affected by foodborne illnesses every year.

REGULATORY AGENCIES

Unsafe food and the diseases related to it have become a major concern for all the countries in the world. To cope with this problem, many regulatory agencies have been set up worldwide. These agencies deal with food-related problems and also prepare guidelines for the food industry. Some of these agencies are the World Health Organization (WHO), the World Food Safety Organization (WFSO), and the European Food Safety Authority (EFSA).

WORDS TO UNDERSTAND

MALNUTRITION: a lack of proper nutrition

OBJECTIVE: the basic goal or purpose of any activity

PHARMACEUTICAL: any activity related to sale of medicines

RLD HEALTH ORGANIZATION (WHO)

HO is the main organization that deals with the health problems of the world, and as a result, governs the food industry. It is an agency of the United Nations (UN). Although it mainly deals with health problems, the close relation between food and health makes it important for the food industry. The WHO has 193 member nations, and its main **objective** is to achieve the highest possible level of health for the entire population of the world.

FOOD AND AGRICULTURE ORGANIZATION OF THE UNITED NATIONS (FAO)

This is another specialized agency of the UN, which was created to deal with the issue of hunger. It is also one of the main agencies that regulates the food industry. This organization is constantly involved in efforts taken to end hunger. The FAO has also undertaken many measures like improving food conditions, dealing with food crises, issuing guidelines for food awareness, and making efforts to reduce **malnutrition**.

EUROPEAN FOOD SAFETY AUTHORITY (EFSA)

In 2002, the European Union (EU) established a regulatory agency to deal with their food problems. This agency was called the European Food Safety Authority (EFSA). It deals with both animal and plant health and welfare. Although it is an independent agency, it receives funds from the EU to carry out its activities.

FOOD SAFETY AND STANDARDS AUTHORITY OF INDIA

Some regulatory agencies govern the entire world, whereas some deal with a single country only. The Food Safety and Standards Authority of India regulates and deals only with the food safety problems of India. This agency works under the Ministry of Health and Family Welfare of India. It was created by the Food Safety and Standards Act (2006). This agency has five regional offices in India. It is led by a chairperson who is appointed by the central government.

STATE FOOD AND DRUG ADMINISTRATION

Another famous regulatory agency is the State Food and Drug Administration of China. It comes under the State Council of the People's Republic of China, and serves all the functions related to food safety, with the goal of improving food conditions and health. However, it does not regulate the ingredients used by pharmaceutical companies.

DID YOU KNOW?

- Most regulatory organizations are governed by the parliaments of their countries.

FOOD SAFETY FOR INDIVIDUALS

Food spoilage means the *deterioration* of food that makes it unsafe for consumption. Food can spoil at any step of food processing. There are some *precautions* that we as individuals can take to keep our food healthy. This small effort can greatly reduce spoilage of food and the diseases caused by it. These measures should be taken while preparing, purchasing, storing, and eating food.

 WORDS TO UNDERSTAND

DETERIORATION: a decline in quality
PRECAUTION: actions designed to prevent or avoid harm
PULSES: peas, beans, and lentils

BUYING SAFE FOOD

There are many things that should be kept in mind when shopping for food. Things like manufacturing and expiration date of products, ingredients, freshness of the items, and packing conditions should be checked before purchasing. Buy food items from those grocery stores that keep fresh products. Food items should also be properly carried back home to avoid spoilage.

COOKING FOOD SAFELY

Food needs proper care during its preparation to reduce the risk of food poisoning. All fruits, vegetables, cereals, and **pulses** should be washed properly before cooking. Many fruits and vegetables can develop bacteria if they are left to sit out too long after chopping. For healthy and safe cooking, the work area, chopping boards, cooking utensils, and kitchen surroundings should be kept clean and dry.

SAFE CONSUMPTION OF FOOD

Food should also be eaten with proper care. As our hands come in physical contact with many things, they may carry bacteria. Hence, the first safety step is to wash your hands properly before touching food. The utensils used while eating food as well as the dining area should also be clean.

SAFE STORAGE OF FOOD

Storing food properly is an extremely important part of food safety. Food usually spoils during storage. Food storage is very important for the food manufacturing industry as well. Different foods need to be stored at different temperatures. Any shortcomings in storage can damage food easily. Time is also an important factor while storing food. Food items should be stored quickly, as any delay may harm their quality.

IMPORTANCE OF FOOD SAFETY FOR INDIVIDUALS

There are many foodborne diseases that can affect us if food is not handled and stored with the necessary precautions in mind. In severe cases, poor quality of food can prove fatal. We should be very cautious in ensuring that the food we are consuming is perfectly safe and healthy.

DID YOU KNOW?

- Sponges and dishrags hold the largest number of germs in the kitchen.
- Food should cool down properly before being stored in a refrigerator.

CATEGORY	FOOD	SAFE MINIMUM COOKING TEMPERATURE (°F)	REST TIME
Ground meat & meat mixtures	Beef, pork, veal, lamb	160°F (70°C)	None
	Turkey, chicken	165°F (75°C)	None
Beef, veal, lamb	Steaks, roasts, chops	145°F (65°C)	3 minutes
Poultry	Chicken & turkey, whole	165°F (75°C)	None
	Poultry breasts, roasts	165°F (75°C)	None
	Poultry thighs, legs, wings	165°F (75°C)	None
	Duck & goose	165°F (75°C)	None
	Stuffing (cooked alone or in bird)	165°F (75°C)	None
Pork & ham	Fresh pork	145°F (65°C)	3 minutes
	Fresh ham (raw)	145°F (65°C)	3 minutes
	Precooked ham (to reheat)	140°F (60°C)	None
Eggs & egg dishes	Eggs	Cook until yolk and white are firm.	None
	Egg dishes	160°F (70°C)	None
Leftovers & casseroles	Leftovers	165°F (75°C)	None
	Casseroles	165°F (75C)	None
Seafood	Fin fish	145°F (65°C), or cook until flesh is opaque and separates easily with a fork.	None
	Shrimp, lobster, and crabs	Cook until flesh is pearly and opaque.	None
	Clams, oysters, and mussels	Cook until shells open during cooking.	None
	Scallops	Cook until flesh is milky white, or opaque and firm.	None

Source: "Safe Minimum Cooking Temperatures," FoodSafety.gov,
https://www.foodsafety.gov/keep/charts/mintemp.html.

31

FOOD SAFETY FOR BUSINESSES

Food safety at businesses is a must since it not only improves one's brand value but also ensures the safety of customers. Places serving food to people are also legally bound to provide good-quality food. They may have to pay huge **compensation** if their customers contract any foodborne illness by consuming their food. Despite such regulations, most of the cases of food poisoning occur due to food consumed from such places.

 ## WORDS TO UNDERSTAND

BUFFET: a meal in which food is put out and guests serve themselves

COMPENSATION: something received or paid due to a loss caused

EXPIRATION DATE: the ending of a particular period; for example, the end of a period when food is safe to eat

FOOD SAFETY AT RESTAURANTS

Most of us don't think much about food safety when going out for meals. However, it is a very important health concern. Many things need to be checked before dining in a restaurant. Cleanliness of the restaurant, the dining area and utensils, the bathroom, and the kitchen should be checked to determine the hygiene level of any place. Restaurants deal with a large quantity of wasted food daily, and there are times when such food is served to customers. Therefore, one must be careful to consume only freshly cooked food in restaurants.

SAFETY OF TAKEOUT FOOD

In places where food is served only over a counter, determining the hygiene level becomes difficult. These places have less space, which may lead to cleanliness problems in some cases. However, the good news is that due to less space, the prepared food is not stored for long. These places generally serve fresh food only, which takes care of at least one very important health concern.

Government health inspectors usually provide some sort of "grade" to let customers know how well a restaurant is doing in terms of cleanliness. In New York City, for example, restaurants must post their grade in a highly visible spot, so that customers know what they are getting into.

FOOD SAFETY AT GROCERY STORES

It's important that grocery stores observe the rules for proper storage of food, because they keep food in huge quantities and for longer periods. Different types of food items are available in grocery stores, ranging from fresh fruits and vegetables to packed and frozen products. All these items have different storage needs. The level of cleanliness of grocery stores can also affect food quality.

Shoppers should check food products before purchasing them, and only items that look fresh should be bought. Also, check the **expiration date** of packaged foods before making the purchase.

FOOD SAFETY AT PARTIES

Food consumed during parties also needs a lot of care. It can sometimes spoil due to the long hours of serving. If a **buffet** system is used, be aware that food kept for more than four hours can become harmful for consumption. The serving area can also affect the quality of food. Food that is served in open areas can be affected by insects, temperature disturbances, and other factors.

Learn about the steps taken by restaurants to keep their food safe.

Safety Food Storage for Commercial Kitchens
1. The FIFO Rule
2. Store Meat Below Other Items
3. Food Should Be Stored In Air Tight Containers
4. Store Food off The Floor

www.kitchen-monkey

FOOD SAFETY AT WAREHOUSES

Warehouses are the places where food gets stored before distribution to grocery stores. Hence, warehouses are also responsible for ensuring food safety. Although storage is an important part, safe transportation of food is also important for them. Any damage to food during loading or unloading should be avoided.

DID YOU KNOW?

- An outbreak of foodborne illness can cost a restaurant anywhere from thousands to millions of dollars in lost revenue.

- The Centers for Disease Control and Prevention (CDC) has estimated that slightly less than half of all foodborne illness cases are caused by food eaten in restaurants.

SAFETY MEASURES FOR FOOD MANUFACTURING

Food production is the first step of the food **supply chain**. *It is one of the most important stages of food safety.*

 ## WORDS TO UNDERSTAND

IRRIGATION: process that gets water to crops to aid growth

PROCESSED: describes something that has gone through a series of operations to change it in some way

SUPPLY CHAIN: a series of processes that are involved in the creation of products

FOOD SAFETY AT FARMS

Food is grown on farms, and even industry-produced food is also dependent on farm foods for raw materials. Many measures must be taken to protect food from spoilage in farms. Food items in farms are affected mainly by natural disasters, low rainfall, insects, pests, and rodents. Many artificial products such as insecticides, pesticides, and methods such as artificial **irrigation** are used to improve food production. However, if these products are used excessively, they might damage the crops.

FOOD SAFETY AT FACTORIES

Factories are also involved in producing food. There are many food items that cannot be used for human consumption unless they are **processed**. Take wheat, for example. Wheat has to be turned into flour, and then the flour can be used to make all kinds of foods, from bread to cereal to pasta.

Food is produced in huge quantities in factories, so it has to be prepared in clean surroundings and with clean machines.

SAFETY MEASURES FOR SMALL-SCALE PRODUCTION

The term *small-scale production* refers to creating food for public use in small community centers and homes. They work at small levels due to the limited availability of location, labor, and resources. Items like pickles, spices, snacks, and sweets are mainly produced by small-scale industries. Cleanliness of surroundings is important for food safety in these places. They should follow all the hygiene guidelines to ensure that food items remain safe during all stages of production.

SAFE PACKAGING OF FOOD

Proper packaging of food is very important to ensure its safety. The food industry is obligated to meet many legal and regulatory requirements while packing food items. The packaging should also be able to protect food from wetness, dryness, or other extreme conditions. It should be airtight, watertight, and resistant to steam and odors.

TRANSPORTING FOOD SAFELY

Proper packing of food protects it from getting damaged during transportation. However, safe handling of food during transportation is also very important. During transportation, food can be affected by external factors, such as environmental changes, accidents, and time taken during transportation. Only food-grade containers should be used for the transportation of food.

DID YOU KNOW?

- Organic farming reduces carbon emissions as compared to industrialized agriculture.

- A major piece of U.S. legislation that regulates food safety during transport is called the Sanitary Transportation of Human and Animal Food.

SAFE TEMPERATURES

Temperature is one of the most important factors affecting food safety. Some food items are consumed raw*, while many others must be cooked before eating. All food items require temperature control. However, some may require it during storage, whereas others require it at cooking and other related stages. Storage of food items should also be done keeping in mind their specific temperature requirements.*

WORDS TO UNDERSTAND

CONSUMPTION: eating something
RAW: uncooked

HEATING AND COOLING OF FOOD ITEMS

Food items are generally heated during the process of cooking. Cooking not only improves the taste of a food item, but also destroys the harmful bacteria contained in it by maintaining a safe internal temperature.

The process of cooling is used for cold foods. Some food items can be prepared by this method while some are preserved by cooling it. For example, ice creams and cold desserts are prepared by cooling whereas fruits and vegetables are stored by cooling.

WHY DOES TEMPERATURE CONTROL MATTER?

Safe temperature is an extremely important concept in protecting food from spoilage. Food items that are believed to have any harmful bacteria should be cooked to the right temperature to kill the bacteria present in them. Items that can help growth of bacteria or production of toxins should also be kept under safe temperature.

REHEATING EFFECTS ON FOOD

Reheating of food requires less time and temperature as compared to cooking. In some cases, reheating is also believed to reduce the nutritional value of food.

TEMPERATURE CONTROL REQUIREMENTS

Proper food preparation and storage require keeping the right temperature for food in mind. Food items available at commercial places must maintain food temperature very carefully. Food items available for public consumption must pass through many stages. Food preparation and storage is common both in household food items and items available outside. However, packing and transportation stages increase the maintenance needs of commercial food items.

PRECAUTIONS FOR FOOD PROTECTION

Most of us are not aware of the safe food temperatures. This may lead to food spoilage. We should take precautions to reduce spoilage of food. The most important one is to read the instructions regarding food preparation and storage on their packs and follow them carefully. Cooking and refrigerating also protects food in most cases.

DID YOU KNOW?

- Bacteria can grow quickly in warm or even room-temperature environments.

- Leftover food should be reheated at 165°F.

SAFE MINIMUM INTERNAL TEMPERATURES

PRODUCT	MINIMUM INTERNAL TEMPERATURE & REST TIME
Beef, pork, veal & lamb steaks, chops, roasts	145°F (62.8°C) and allow to rest for at least 3 minutes.
Ground meats	160°F (71.1°C)
Ham, fresh or smoked (uncooked)	145°F (62.8°C) and allow to rest for at least 3 minutes.
Fully cooked ham (to reheat)	Reheat cooked hams packaged in USDA-inspected plants to 140°F (60°C) and all others to 165°F (73.9°C).

PRODUCT	MINIMUM INTERNAL TEMPERATURE
Poultry (breasts, whole bird, legs, thighs, and wings, ground poultry, and stuffing)	165°F (73.9°C)
Eggs	160°F (71.1°C)
Fish & shellfish	145°F (62.8°C)
Leftovers	165°F (73.9°C)
Casseroles	165°F (73.9°C)

Source: U.S. Department of Agriculture, Food Inspection and Safety Service, "Safe Minimum Temperature Chart," https://www.fsis.usda.gov/wps/portal/fsis/topics/food-safety-education/get-answers/food-safety-fact-sheets/safe-food-handling/safe-minimum-internal-temperature-chart/ct_index.

TIME FACTOR

Time plays a very important role in the safety of food items. The time factor is crucial, for example, when cooking meat to a specific temperature, or when determining how long milk can be stored safely. Duration *is important right from the stage of food production to the preparatory stage and the storage of food. Food items tend to spoil after a certain period of time. However, with proper food storage and food preservation methods, we can increase this duration.*

 WORDS TO UNDERSTAND

DURATION: describes how long something goes on

HARVESTING: the process of collecting crops when they are ready for use

SOWING: to spread seeds for growing crops

PRODUCTION TIME OF FOOD ITEMS

The first stage of the food cycle is its production. A food item can be produced in either farms or factories. In both cases, the duration of production is important. In agriculture, food items get ready for use in a set period of time. Time here is divided into categories like **sowing** time, standing time, and **harvesting** time. In factories also, food products go through the production process, which takes a definite period of time.

COOKING TIME AND ITS EFFECTS

The preparation stage of food also needs the investment of time. Different food items require different amounts of cooking time. In fact, the method of cooking determines the cooking time required for any dish. For example, roasting, baking, or grilling may take more time compared to steaming, heating, or frying. Cooking time also depends on the temperature at which the food is being cooked. If it is cooked at a very low temperature, the cooking time required to get the dish ready increases.

REST TIME

The time given to a food item after removing it from a heat source and before eating it is called rest time. Rest time is important in the process of preparing food. For example, steaks should be allowed to "rest" after grilling to allow the cooking process to finish. The temperature of a food item changes during the rest time. It decreases in hot dishes and increases in cold ones.

TIME HOLDS THE KEY

If food is kept in poor conditions for long periods of time, it can become unsafe for consumption. Hence, it must be ensured that once you have finished eating, any leftovers should be stored in a refrigerator to prevent the food from spoiling. Ironically, you do need to wait until leftovers have completely cooled before putting them in the refrigerator. Refrigerating still-warm food can encourage bacteria growth.

PRESERVING FOOD FROM EXPIRATION

All food items remain fresh and healthy for a certain period of time. This makes the expiration date, or the manufacturing date, mentioned on the packs of food items important. Refrigerating food items can increase their lifespan, but even then, they won't last very long. However, these days, food preservation has increased the life of food products to a relatively longer span of time.

DID YOU KNOW?

- Overcooking can lead to loss of nutrients.

- Grains can spoil if they are not harvested in time.

FOOD SAFETY MANAGEMENT SYSTEM

In order to practice food safety, many management systems have been designed all over the world. Most of these systems are aimed at developing preventive methods of food safety. The most significant is the Hazard Analysis *Critical* Control Point system (HACCP), which is accepted and used in almost all parts of the world. The principles of HACCP form the basis of most food safety and quality systems.

WORDS TO UNDERSTAND

CRITICAL: describes issues or points that need special attention

EVALUATING: the process of judging something by checking all its related factors

MINIMIZING: reducing something to the least possible level

WHAT IS HACCP?

HACCP is a system of identifying, **evaluating**, and controlling any harmful biological, physical, or chemical agents that hamper food safety. Since this system is followed in many places, it gives a sense of safety to consumers. It aims at **minimizing** the causes of food spoilage.

The HACCP system follows seven principles. The first principle involves conducting a hazard analysis. The second is determining the Critical Control Points (CCPs). The third principle involves establishing critical limits. The fourth principle is about monitoring the control of the critical points. The fifth principle is establishing the corrective action needed. The sixth principle is forming procedures to check the functioning of this system. The seventh principle deals with maintaining records about the functioning of this system.

HACCP APPLICATION RANGE

The HACCP system applies to a variety of food categories, such as seafood, the animal meat industry, organic chemical contaminants, and bulk dairy production. Among agricultural products, some of the items monitored by the HACCP are cereals, dried fruits, nuts, and coffee beans. In the United States, the application range of the HACCP includes fresh-cut produce, juice and nectar products, food outlets, school food and services.

IMPORTANCE OF HACCP

Basic precautions to protect food from spoilage can be taken by everyone. However, companies that produce mass quantities of food are legally bound to follow more rigorous food-safety measures. Places that sell food items fall under this category. The HACCP plan has now become compulsory for many such organizations. Organizations dealing with food preservation activities like smoking, curing, adding preservatives, and canning also need to follow the HACCP guidelines.

BENEFITS OF HACCP

Among the many benefits of the HACCP system, the most important is the use and improvement of safety and quality control methods across all segments of the food industry. This helps ensure consumers that their food is safe and of good quality. It has also reduced errors that result in food spoilage, and has improved the working conditions and practices in the food industry.

PRACTICING THE HACCP SYSTEM

To start a HACCP system, a company must first write a HACCP plan. Companies may use generic models as resources for developing a plant specific plan, however, the most useful and successful HACCP plans need to be developed from the very beginning from the plant that will use and implement the plan. To develop a HACCP plan, a team of individuals from within the company, with some assistance from outside experts, conducts five preliminary steps and applies the seven HACCP principles.

DID YOU KNOW?

- HACCP was first used by meat and poultry companies. However, it later came to be used for other products as well.

- HACCP certification can be issued to businesses only, not to individuals.

FOOD PRESERVATION

The objective of food preservation is to maintain the taste, texture, smell, color, and nutritional value of food items. Methods of food preservation include smoking, salting, canning, drying, and freezing. All these methods aim at preserving food by removing or controlling the growth of harmful organisms like bacteria, fungi, and others. However, some nutrients can spoil during the process of preservation.

 WORDS TO UNDERSTAND

ACIDS: chemical substances present in food

MICROORGANISMS: tiny life forms such as bacteria

PRESSURE: continuous physical force applied to something

WHY PRESERVE FOOD?

Food preservation is required to protect food from spoiling before use. There are basically two causes of food spoilage. The first is the presence or formation of harmful organisms in food. The second is the destruction of essential nutrients or compounds present in food. Spoilage can occur at any stage of the food cycle, such as production, storage, or consumption.

PRESSURE TECHNIQUE

Pressure can be used effectively for the preservation of food. In this method, containers of food items are exposed to very high pressure, which destroys harmful organisms present in them. The removal of these organisms reduces the chances of food spoilage. The texture, flavor, freshness, look, and nutritional value of food items can be maintained by using the pressure technique.

AIR AND MOISTURE

The air and moisture present in the atmosphere can greatly affect food items in many ways. Airtight containers came into use to guard food against the negative effects of atmosphere. However, atmospheric elements can be helpful in preservation of food if used in a controlled way. Many atmospheric elements like oxygen, carbon dioxide, and nitrogen are used effectively to preserve food. These methods of preserving food items are used mostly for grains.

EFFECT OF MICROORGANISMS IN PRESERVATION

Microorganisms are believed to be responsible for spoiling food. However, some microorganisms help in preserving food. These organisms produce certain **acids** that reduce the possibility of the growth of harmful organisms in food. They also produce good living conditions for those organisms that help in keeping the food healthy for humans. Nowadays, specially controlled conditions are created to preserve food by this method. Items like wine, beer, and cheese are preserved by this process.

THE NECESSITY OF FOOD PRESERVATION

With passing time, food preservation has become a necessity. Due to the increased demand for food worldwide, it is essential to preserve food to protect it from spoilage. The shortage of food in the world also makes its preservation important. The growing importance of the preservation of food has emphasized the importance of preservatives in the food industry.

DID YOU KNOW?

- Coffee is preserved by the process of dehydration or drying.

- Salting helps in preserving many meat products. It is one of the oldest methods of food preservation.

- Vinegar helps in the preservation of pickles.

METHODS OF FOOD PRESERVATION

In earlier times, food was preserved only on a very small scale. However, now people consume food from all regions, which has caused food preservation to become an industry. There are many methods used in food preservation. Traditional methods are those that have been used since ancient times and are successful without any scientific guidance. They also include many natural methods of preservation. Scientific methods of preservation have been developed after a lot of research.

frozen vegetable

fish & shrimp

mango & papaya

WORDS TO UNDERSTAND

HUMIDITY: the amount of water vapor in the air

STERILIZE: the process of killing biological agents like bacteria and viruses

VACUUM DRYING: a process of food preservation in which air pressure is greatly reduced, which causes faster drying

SMOKING

The method of using smoke from wood for preventing food spoilage is called smoking. Smoking also enhances the flavor of certain food items. This method was discovered accidentally by people in earlier times. In this method, food is preserved either by hot smoking or cold smoking. Hot smoking is used for frozen foods, and cold smoking is used for salted food items. Humidity, airspeed, the quantity of salt in the product, and the time involved in smoking increase the effectiveness of this method.

DRYING

Drying is a natural method of preserving food. In this method, the moisture content of the food is removed by drying it. Food items can be naturally dried by the actions of the sun or the air. Nowadays, many artificial methods are also used for drying. Vacuum drying, freeze-drying, and using fans and heaters are some of these artificial methods. However, many nutrients can be lost during artificial drying.

FREEZING

The process of preserving food by storing it at extremely low temperatures is called freezing. Food items are lowered to reach their freezing points so that they can be preserved for a long period of time. This process is effective as harmful organisms cannot grow at very low temperatures. However, as in the case of boiling, the organisms present in the food are not killed by freezing.

Learn about how salt preserves meat.

SALTING

Adding salt to prevent food spoilage is one of the oldest methods of food preservation. This method also uses the method of drying for the preservation of food. Salt acts as a drying agent, binding the molecules of water together. High levels of salt in food slows the growth of harmful organisms. Salt solutions and injections are now also used to preserve food. Sugar has a similar effect on food items and is also a popular preservative.

CANNING

The method of preserving food in bottles or cans is called canning. In this process, food items are treated before they are stored in sterilized cans and bottles. The food stays protected in these cans until the cans are opened. Preservatives are also added to food items that are stored this way.

DID YOU KNOW?

- Those canned foods that contain high levels of acids should not be stored for a long time.

- Fruits can be preserved in the form of jams and jellies.

- Botulism is a bacterium that can grow in food items that are not canned properly.

FOOD PROCESSING

Not all food items produced on farms can be consumed in their raw forms. Many must be converted into a form that makes them easier to cook. The method of converting raw food items into easily usable food products is called food processing. Many techniques and machines are used for this process. Animal products are also converted into easy-use food products by food processing. Food items are also cleaned and preserved in this process.

WORDS TO UNDERSTAND

COMPONENT: something that is a part of a whole

EFFICIENCY: the skill to complete an activity both accurately and quickly

ELEMENT: an important part of some item or process

ORIGIN OF FOOD PROCESSING

In earlier times, food was processed by using natural and traditional methods. Food processing was not a very big industry. Food used to be processed either in houses or on a small scale. The concept of easy-cook food developed due to the lack of time. As people became busier in their professional lives, they started looking for foods that could be prepared easily. Processed food was first used for the military, as they did not have proper cooking means. With passing time, easy-cook food items became popular.

FOOD-PROCESSING METHODS

Food processing aims at making food safe, improving its quality, and ensuring its availability in easily usable forms. Many methods are used for processing food. Basic methods of food processing are baking, pasteurization, mixing, heat transfer, among others. As food must be made safe, food preservation is also considered when it is being processed. Some methods of food preservation like smoking, salting, drying, freezing, sugaring, and pickling are also used when processing food.

ELEMENTS OF FOOD PROCESSING

There are four basic **elements** that are important in food processing. The first element is hygiene. This deals with cleanliness in the food processing method. The second element is health, which aims at maintaining the healthy **components** of food items while they are processed. The third element is **efficiency,** which includes proper use of machines and labor. The fourth element is minimizing waste. Food should be processed using methods that reduce waste.

WHY PROCESS FOOD?

There are many benefits of food processing. The most important benefit is the improvement of taste and quality. The life of food products also increases as the risk of spoilage is reduced. This aids in transportation of food and increases its availability. Because food is processed in huge quantities, the cost of converting it from raw form to consumable form at home is reduced.

DOWNSIDES OF FOOD PROCESSING

Like all the other methods, food processing also has its share of downsides. The loss of nutrients while the food is processed is the main disadvantage of this process. Adding artificial preservatives is also not considered good for human health. Because food touches many containers and machines during this process, the risk of its spoiling can also increase in some cases.

DID YOU KNOW?

- Some artificial additives are good for maintaining the quality of food. However, the safety of some additives has also been questioned.

- Some processed food items are more nutritious than their raw forms.

FOOD STORAGE

Storing food is one of the most important parts of the food cycle. It is used for both raw and processed food items. Storage is also important for items that are cooked for final use. When food is transported from one place to another, it should be handled and stored properly to avoid damage. Some food items must be used throughout the year, but they are produced only at a particular time of the year. These items must also be stored for future use.

WORDS TO UNDERSTAND

AIRTIGHT: describes a container or packaging that does not allow air to get in

EXPOSED: unprotected

PRECAUTION: care taken in advance to protect something

STORING FOOD AT HOME

It is possible to use food items for a long period of time if they are stored safely. The quantity of these food items determines the methods that can be used for storing them. Different types of cereals, pulses, spices, and herbs can be stored for long periods at home. Because they are already processed, they can be easily stored in clean, **airtight** plastic containers. Most cooked food items are preserved via refrigeration.

STORING FOOD AT COMMERCIAL PLACES

Huge quantities of food items are stored at commercial places like supermarkets and restaurants. These places use special containers and methods for storing food. However, most of these methods are similar to those used in homes. Freezers, plastic and metal containers, and bags are what are mostly used in these places. Storing food items for transportation is also done by the food industry, as this requires more care and **precaution** to ensure the foods remain safe.

WHY STORE FOOD?

Food storage is important since it helps to fulfill people's food requirements. Storage allows availability of food at all times. It also reduces the wasting and spoiling of food. As food shortage is a major problem, proper storage helps to deal with this to a certain extent. It also provides us with a variety of food items, as they can be transported easily.

HANDLING FOOD FOR STORAGE

Many things need to be remembered when handling food for storage. Fruits and vegetables should be refrigerated without much delay. This increases their life. The items that must be frozen should be stored at or below 0°F (-18°C). Food items need to be wrapped properly before storage so they are not **exposed** to oxygen.

DID YOU KNOW?

- Be sure to check food labels for storage information and follow the instructions.

- Refrigerators should be set at or below 40°F (4°C) to reduce the growth of bacteria.

FOODBORNE DISEASES

Foodborne diseases are mostly caused by consuming contaminated food. The quality and condition of food is very important if we want to avoid illnesses caused by the contamination of food. All food items should be checked properly before consumption, because its poor condition may lead to disease.

 WORDS TO UNDERSTAND

DEHYDRATION: a condition where the body lacks sufficient water

IMMUNE SYSTEM: the system, including the spleen and lymph nodes, that helps the body fight off diseases

PREVENTION OF FOODBORNE DISEASES

Most of the causes of food spoilage can be controlled. If these causes are controlled properly, many cases of foodborne diseases can be prevented. The most important way to prevent these diseases is by maintaining hygienic surroundings. Cooking food properly can kill most germs. Handling food at proper temperatures also reduces the chances of food spoilage. Washing food items properly can also prevent such problems.

WHAT CAUSES FOODBORNE DISEASES?

Bacteria, fungi, viruses, and parasites are the main causes of food spoilage. They can spoil the food at any level of the food cycle. The food cycle includes many processes like production, transportation, processing, and storage. Food can be contaminated at any of these stages due to poor handling.

SYMPTOMS OF FOODBORNE DISEASES

The symptoms of foodborne diseases vary and, depending on the nature of illness, can be mild or severe. Most of these

symptoms are related to the problems experienced in the digestion of food. The most important symptom is the weakening of the body's **immune system,** making the body vulnerable to illness. Other symptoms include vomiting, nausea, fever, **dehydration**, fatigue, and headache. Hunger may also be affected.

TREATMENT

Treatment of foodborne illnesses varies depending on the specific type of illness. Most cases of foodborne diseases will resolve on their own. Consumption of light foods and increasing the intake of fluids can treat mild cases of foodborne diseases. Some cases may also need light medication. However, occasionally there are situations where illness is quite serious and requires treatment.

DID YOU KNOW?

- The CDC estimates that about 48 million Americans contract foodborne illnesses every year.

- There are around 250 types of foodborne diseases.

COMMON FOODBORNE GERMS

- Campylobacter
- *Clostridium botulinum*
- *Clostridium perfringens*
- *Escherichia coli* (E. coli)
- Listeria
- Norovirus
- Salmonella
- *Staphylococcus aureus*
- Vibrio

WATERBORNE DISEASES

Water is a very important part of our diet. We simply cannot live without water. Water is used in many activities and is available in many forms. Water available in natural forms includes seawater, river water, rainwater, and water present in glaciers. All these water forms can become contaminated due to human activities.

 **WORDS TO UNDERSTAND**

GASTROENTERITIS: an illness that causes inflammation of the stomach and intestines

POTABLE: drinkable

RESPIRATORY: the bodily system that controls breathing

INFECTION FROM BACTERIA

Microorganisms can be found every-where and can contaminate water. Consumption of contaminated water can lead to several diseases in humans. Some diseases caused by bacterial infection in water are typhoid fever, botulism, cholera, dysentery, and salmonella. Common symptoms of these diseases are diarrhea, weakness in the body, vomiting, fever, and nausea. Diseases caused by water contami-nation need proper treatment.

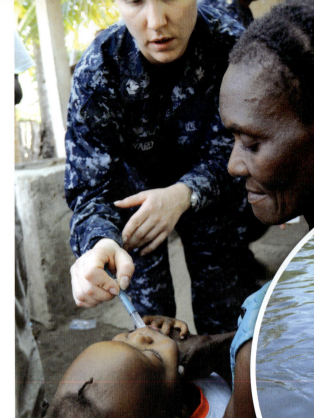

SOURCES OF WATERBORNE DISEASES

It is understood that the chief source of waterborne diseases is contami-nated water. However, contaminated water can affect us in many ways since we use water for several purposes. Drinking contaminated water can be life threatening, as can eating food prepared from such water. Using infected water for washing clothes, bathing, preparing food, and other such purposes can also cause infections.

VIRAL CONTAMINATION

Viruses also commonly cause contamination of water. The diseases caused due to contamination by viruses can be very harmful in some cases. Common diseases caused by the viral contamination of water are **gastroenteritis**, hepatitis A, polyomavirus infection, and severe acute **respiratory** syndrome. Some symptoms of these diseases are fatigue, fever, headache, nausea, diarrhea, and respiratory problems. The symptoms are generally the same for all kinds of infections caused by the viral contamination of water.

WATER CONTAMINATION FROM PARASITES

Parasites can also contaminate water. The use of water contaminated by parasites can cause diseases even when it is not consumed directly. It can cause harm even when the contaminated water is used for other purposes. Some diseases caused by parasitic contamination of water are schistosomiasis, taeniasis, coenurosis, and enterobiasis. Symptoms of these diseases are fever, cough, rash, allergy, vomiting, problems in the liver and intestine, and diarrhea. These diseases can be very dangerous to human health.

EFFECTS OF WATERBORNE DISEASES

The diseases caused by water have several effects. Since water is consumed on a very large scale, its contamination affects a population of people. Widespread illness is one of the most harmful effects of such diseases. A huge amount of money is needed for treatment. However, it is not always possible for everyone to manage the finances required for treatment. In some cases, waterborne diseases can even result in death.

DID YOU KNOW?

- Seventy percent of the Earth's surface is covered by water, but only around two percent of that water is potable.

- About 780 million people do not have access to an improved water resource.

FOOD ALLERGIES

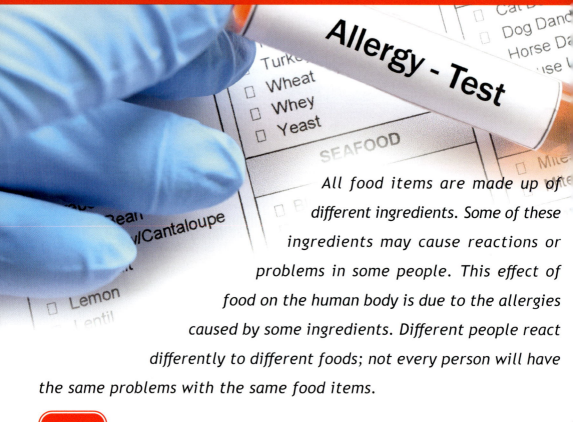

All food items are made up of different ingredients. Some of these ingredients may cause reactions or problems in some people. This effect of food on the human body is due to the allergies caused by some ingredients. Different people react differently to different foods; not every person will have the same problems with the same food items.

WORDS TO UNDERSTAND

ANALYZE: to examine something in detail using various methods

LACTOSE: a type of sugar that some people have trouble digesting

PROTEIN: a type of compound that is vital to human functioning

TYPES OF FOOD ALLERGY

There are some specific foods that are known to cause allergy, such as eggs, peanuts, milk, fish, strawberries, tomatoes, soy, and nuts. Children are more vulnerable to allergic reactions caused by peanuts, eggs, soy, and milk, whereas adults are susceptible to allergies caused by citrus fruits, wheat, nuts, and fish. Ninety percent of food allergies are caused by the foods just mentioned.

WHAT CAUSES FOOD ALLERGIES?

Our body tries to defend us from any possible harm. Any intake of harmful substance can be sensed by the body and the immune system responds. However, sometimes our body also reacts negatively to a harmless food item. This response is an allergic reaction. This allergy is caused by the presence of an allergy-producing substance called Immunoglobulin E. Food allergies are rarely caused by preservatives or food additives.

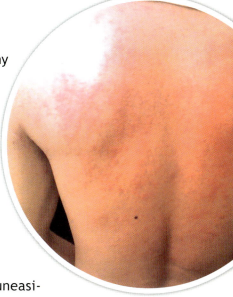

SYMPTOMS OF FOOD ALLERGIES

An allergic reaction often begins with a feeling of uneasiness immediately after consuming the item one is allergic to.
The body starts reacting within two hours of eating such a food item. Common symptoms of food allergy are vomiting, nausea, diarrhea, nasal congestion, stomach

A short video about how food allergies impact students.

infections, and breathing problems. In some cases, the blood pressure can also become low. The throat can also become infected. Symptoms vary for different allergies.

TREATMENT OF FOOD ALLERGIES

Medicines are given only to ease the reactions caused by allergies. The food items that cause problems must be avoided. As is true of other diseases, before receiving any treatment for allergies, a person is tested. There are three types of tests for food allergies: a skin-prick test, a blood test, and a food challenge. A food challenge involves administering the same food that one is allergic to in a controlled way to **analyze** the reaction.

OTHER FOOD REACTIONS

Sometimes people have physical reactions to food that don't qualify as actual allergies. One example of a nonallergic reaction is **lactose** intolerance. People with this condition have difficulty digesting dairy products. But it's not an allergic reaction—instead, lactose intolerance stems from an absence of lactase, the **protein** the body uses to break down the lactose in dairy products.

DID YOU KNOW?

- People with food allergies are more likely to suffer from asthma.

- Peanut allergy is the most common allergy in the United States.

MYTHS AND FACTS

People make many efforts to protect their food. What we don't know is that since our ways of food preservation have been in use over time, they have almost become facts. However, there are certain myths associated with the safety of food. Some of the measures for keeping our food safe may not be as effective as some people think.

MYTH: IT IS NOT NECESSARY TO WASH FRUITS AND VEGETABLES THAT HAVE TO BE PEELED.

This is one of the most popular food beliefs, that washing a fruit or vegetable won't make any difference if the outer peel has to be removed before consumption. However, this is not true. The outer peel is home to various bacteria and chemicals. These impurities can be easily transferred to the inner portion of our food during the process of peeling.

MYTH: LOW-CALORIE SWEETENERS CAUSE CANCER.

Food items prepared artificially are easily seen as disease-causing products. Low-calorie sweeteners are no exception. The link between low-calorie sweeteners and cancer was assumed since the introduction of this product. But despite many studies on the issue, no evidence has come to light that low-calorie sweeteners are responsible for causing cancer.

MYTH: ALL FOOD ADDITIVES ARE ARTIFICIAL.

This is another popular food belief. All additives are assumed to be artificial in nature. However, this is not true. Fruits and vegetables are the most common source of food additives. Their seeds, fruits, and other parts are used in making many thickening agents. Edible oils and organic acids are also natural products that are processed to be used as additives.

MYTH: PROCESSED FOODS ARE ALWAYS UNHEALTHY.

Some people believe that processed food items are treated with chemical additives and artificial methods and that they lose all their nutrition in this process. However, this belief is not completely true. Many processed food items have been discovered to be as healthy as natural food.

MYTH: TO THAW FROZEN MEAT, JUST LEAVE IT OUT ON THE COUNTER.

People often assume that because it takes time for meat to thaw, there is lots of time before bacteria starts to grow. But there are a few things you should consider. First, meat thaws from the outside in, meaning that the outer part of the meat is sitting at room temperature even when the inside is still frozen. Second, bacteria grow surprisingly quickly at room temperature; contamination can happen much sooner than you think.

DID YOU KNOW?

- A can opener should be washed thoroughly after each use.

- Food that doesn't look or smell bad can still be spoiled.

TEXT-DEPENDENT QUESTIONS

1. What are the main causes of food spoilage?

2. What can be done to prevent biological hazards?

3. What are some examples of chemical hazards?

4. What is an example of a food-safety regulation law?

5. What global organizations help regulate food safety?

6. What are some of the symptoms of food poisoning?

7. What are some of the bacteria that can cause food poisoning?

8. What are some examples of waterborne diseases?

9. Why do food allergies happen?

10. Why is it a bad idea to let meat thaw on the counter?

1. Select a foodborne illness from this book and find out more about its causes, symptoms, and treatment.

2. Using this text and other sources, find out more about what steps people can take to limit their exposure to foodborne illnesses. Make a list of tips and turn it into a poster or pamphlet.

3. There are a variety of things that cause more than their share of diseases, such as contaminated water, spoiled food, and chemical contamination. Choose one of these or some other that interests you and study how it occurs and what can be done about it. Write a report on what ought to be done in the future to limit these problems.

4. Do some research on government regulations. Besides the laws mentioned in the text, what are some rules and laws that try to keep food safe? Write a report on the state of food-safety legislation.

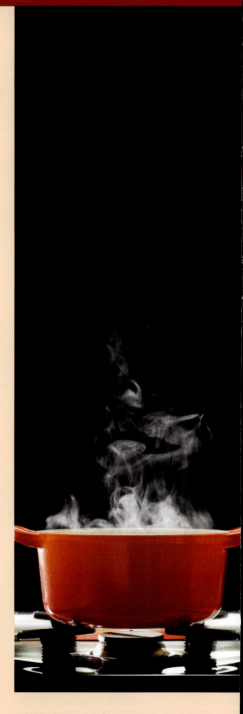

SERIES GLOSSARY OF KEY TERMS

amino acid: an organic molecule that is the building block of proteins.

antibody: a protein in the blood that fights off substances the body thinks are dangerous.

antioxidant: a substance that fights against free radicals, molecules in the body that can damage other cells.

biofortification: the process of improving the nutritional value of crops through breeding or genetic modification.

calories: units of heat used to indicate the amount of energy that foods will produce in the human body.

carbohydrates: substances found in certain foods (such as bread, rice, and potatoes) that provide the body with heat and energy and are made of carbon, hydrogen, and oxygen.

carcinogen: something that causes cancer.

cardiovascular: of or relating to the heart and blood vessels.

carnivorous: meat-eating.

cholesterol: a soft, waxy substance present in all parts of the body, including the skin, muscles, liver, and intestines.

collagen: a fibrous protein that makes up much of the body's connective tissues.

deficiency: a lack of something, such as a nutrient in one's diet.

derivative: a product that is made from another source; for example, malt comes from barley, making it a barley derivative.

diabetes: a disease in which the body's ability to produce the hormone insulin is impaired.

dietary supplements: products taken orally that contain one or more ingredient (such as vitamins or amino acids) that are intended to supplement one's diet and are not considered food.

electrolytes: substances (such as sodium or calcium) that are ions in the body regulating the flow of nutrients into and waste products out of cells.

enzyme: a protein that starts or accelerates an action or process within the body.

flexible: applies to something that can be readily bent, twisted, or folded without any sign of injury.

food additive: a product added to a food to improve flavor, appearance, nutritional value, or shelf life.

genetically modified organism (GMO): a plant or animal that has had its genetic material altered to create new characteristics.

growth hormone: a substance either naturally produced by the body or synthetically made that stimulates growth in animals or plants.

herbicide: a substance designed to kill unwanted plants, such as weeds.

hydration: to supply with ample fluid or moisture.

macronutrients: nutrients required in large amounts for the health of living organisms, including proteins, fats, and carbohydrates.

metabolism: the chemical process by which living cells produce energy.

micronutrients: nutrients required in very small amounts for the health of living organisms.

nutritional profile: the nutritional makeup of given foods, including the balance of vitamins, minerals, proteins, fats, and other components.

obesity: a condition in which excess body fat has amassed to the point where it causes ill-health effects.

pasteurization: a process that kills microorganisms, making certain foods and drinks safer to consume.

pesticide: a substance designed to kill insects or other organisms that can cause damage to plants or animals.

processed food: food that has been refined before resale, often with additional fats, sugars, sodium, and other additives.

protein: a nutrient found in food (as in meat, milk, eggs, and beans) that is made up of many amino acids joined together, is a necessary part of the diet, and is essential for normal cell structure and function.

protein complementation: the dietary practice of combining different plant-based foods to get all of the essential amino acids.

refined: when referring to grains or flours, describing those that have been processed to remove elements of the whole grain.

sustainable: a practice that can be successfully maintained over a long period of time.

vegan: a person who does not eat meat, poultry, fish, dairy, or other products sourced from animals.

vegetarian: a person who does not eat meat, poultry, or fish.

whole grain: grains that have been minimally processed and contain all three main parts of the grain—the bran, the germ, and the endosperm.

workout: a practice or exercise to test or improve one's fitness for athletic competition, ability, or performance.

FURTHER READING

FOOD AND AGRICULTURAL ORGANIZATION. *Food Handler's Handbook.* (Washington, DC: 2017).

PERRITANO, JOHN. *Food Safety. Know Your Food.* (Broomall, PA: Mason Crest, 2017).

REDMAN, NINA E., AND MICHELE MORRONE. *Food Safety: A Reference Handbook.* Contemporary World Issues. (Santa Barbara, CA: ABC-CLIO, 2017).

SHAW, IAN. *Food Safety: The Science of Keeping Food Safe.* (Hoboken, NJ: John Wiley & Sons, 2018).

INTERNET RESOURCES

BASICS FOR HANDLING FOOD SAFETY

This page from the U.S. Department of Agriculture provides a solid introduction to everything you need to know about handling food in as safe a manner as possible.

https://www.fsis.usda.gov/wps/portal/fsis/topics/food-safety-education/get-answers/food-safety-fact-sheets/safe-food-handling/basics-for-handling-food-safely/ct_index

FOODBORNE ILLNESSES AND GERMS

Everything you need to know about foodborne illnesses is available at the CDC's gateway.

https://www.cdc.gov/foodsafety/foodborne-germs.html

FOODSAFETY.GOV

This site, run by the U.S. Department of Health and Human Services, is a gateway to anything you need to know about food safety topics.

https://www.foodsafety.gov/

HOW FAST FOOD WORKS: FAST-FOOD SAFETY AND NUTRITION

This page from How Stuff Works will educate you about food safety issues as they relate to fast food.

https://science.howstuffworks.com/innovation/edible-innovations/fast-food2.htm

INDEX

grilling, 43
grocery stores, 29, 34

H

handwashing, 8, 17, 29
harvest, 42-43
Hazard Analysis Critical Control Point (HAACP) system, 45-47
headache, 62
Health and Human Services (US), 77
health inspectors, 33
heat transfer, 55
hepatitis A rotavirus, 14, 64
high-risk hazards, 20
hygiene, 7-9, 31-33, 56, 61

I

ice cream, 40
immune system, 60, 62
Immunoglobulin E, 67
imported foods, 22-23
impurities, 10-21
industrialized farming, 38
infections, 14, 64-68
insecticides, 37
intestinal problems, 21, 65
irrigation, 36-37

J

jams, 53
jellies, 53
juice products, 46

K

knowledge, 8, 47

L

labelling, 17, 22, 40
lactose intolerance, 66, 68
laws
    projects on, 72
    regulating businesses, 32-33
    regulating food production, 38, 45-47
    regulating foods, 10, 22-27
    See also regulations; regulatory agencies
leftover food, 31, 41
Listeria monocytogenes, 14
liver problems, 65
low-calorie sweeteners, 69

low-risk hazards, 20
lymph nodes, 60

M

malnutrition, 25-26
manufacturing, 23, 36-37
medications, 68
medium-risk hazards, 20
metabolism, 16-17, 20-21
metals, 19-20
microorganisms, 12, 48-50, 52, 62, 64
    See also bacteria; food preservation
microwaves, 9
mixing, 55
modern lifestyles, 7, 55
moisture, 49, 51

N

nails, 20-21
nasal congestion, 67
natural disasters, 37
nausea, 64, 67
nectar products, 46
needles, 20
nitrogen, 49
norovirus, 14
Norwalk virus, 14
nutrition, 7, 9, 40, 44, 48-49, 56, 70
nuts, 46, 67

O

obesity, 8-9
oils, 70
organic farming, 38
oxygen, 49, 59

P

packaged foods, 8, 17-18, 29, 38
parasites, 13-15, 61, 65
parties, 35
pasta, 37
pasteurization, 55
peanuts, 67-68
peeling, 69
personal hygiene, 17
pesticides, 11, 17, 37
pharmaceutical industry, 25, 27
physical hazards, 12, 19-21, 35
pickles, 37
plastics, 19-20

pollution, 17, 63-64
polyomavirus, 64
precautions, 28-31, 40-41, 47
preservatives, 13, 42, 47, 52-53, 56, 67
    See also food preservation
pressure, 49
processed foods, 36, 54-56, 70
proteins, 66, 68
pulses, 28-29

Q

QR Video
    effect of food allergies, 68
    food safety in restaurants, 35
    how salt preserves meat, 52
    introduction to food safety, 7
    toxic chemicals in food, 18

R

rash, 65
raw foods, 39, 53
ready-to-cook foods, 12, 55
refrigeration, 14, 58-59
regulatory agencies, 10, 17, 22-25
respiratory system, 63-64
restaurants, 32-33, 35
roasting, 43

S

Safe Minimum Temperature Charts, 31, 41
safety
    for bulk food, 33-35
    for fast foods, 8
    importance of, 6-8, 30, 47
    management systems for, 45-47
    and preventive measures, 28-31
    and proper washing, 9, 29, 61, 69
    and purchasing choices, 21
    stages of, 6
    temperature and, 31, 39-41, 70
    and time factor, 35, 39-44
    water and, 63-65
    when eating, 29, 35

Photo Credits